Anatomy of the World

Anatomy of the World

Poems

Celia Meade

RESOURCE *Publications* · Eugene, Oregon

ANATOMY OF THE WORLD
Poems

Copyright © 2023 Celia Meade. All rights reserved. Except for brief quotations in critical publications or reviews, no part of this book may be reproduced in any manner without prior written permission from the publisher. Write: Permissions, Wipf and Stock Publishers, 199 W. 8th Ave., Suite 3, Eugene, OR 97401.

Resource Publications
An Imprint of Wipf and Stock Publishers
199 W. 8th Ave., Suite 3
Eugene, OR 97401

www.wipfandstock.com

PAPERBACK ISBN: 978-1-6667-7098-8
HARDCOVER ISBN: 978-1-6667-7099-5
EBOOK ISBN: 978-1-6667-7100-8

VERSION NUMBER 11/06/23

Permissions

Photos of anatomy taken from Wikimedia Commons, "Gray's Anatomy Plates." Public domain.

"The Lumberjack's Dove" by GennaRose Nethercott. Copyright 2018. Used by permission of HarperCollins Publishers.

Tales From Ovid by Ted Hughes. Used by permission of Faber and Faber Ltd.

"Heart" from *Smoke*. Copyright 2000 by Dorianne Laux. Reprinted with the permission of The Permissions Company, LLC on behalf of BOA Editions, Ltd. https://www.boaeditions.org/.

From "End of Winter" from *The Wild Iris* by Louise Gluck. Copyright (c) 1992. Used by permission of HarperCollins Publishers.

"When the War is Over" from *Migration: New and Selected Poems*. Copyright 1969 by M. S. Merwin. Reprinted with the permission of the Permission Company, LLC on behalf of Copper Canyon Press. https://www.coppercanyonpress.org/.

Excerpt from "Family Vacation" by Judith Slater, from *The Wind Turning Pages*, 2011. Reprinted with permission of Judith Slater.

"Ballad" by Dianne Suess, from *Poem-A-Day, Poetry.org*. Reprinted with permission of the author.

"Memory of a Bird" by Linda Pastan, from *Almost an Elegy: New and Later Selected Poems*. Copyright 2022 by Linda Pastan. Used by permission of W. W. Norton & Company, Inc.

"The Delirium Waltz" from *Blizzard of One: Poems* by Mark Strand, copyright 1998 by Mark Strand. Used by permission of Alfred A. Knopf, an imprint of the Knopf Doubleday Publishing Group, a division of Penguin Random House LLC. All rights reserved.

"Night Ferry" by Peter Sacks, from *Natal Command*. Copyright 1997. Used by permission of University of Chicago Press.

"Faith Healing" by Philip Larkin, from *The Whitsun Weddings*. Used by permission of Faber and Faber Ltd.

Pocket Pema Chodron, by Pema Chodron, c. 2008. Reprinted by arrangement with Shambala Publications, Inc. Boulder, CO. https://www.shambhala.com/.

Another Bullshit Night in Suck City: A Memoir by Nick Flynn. Copyright 2004 by Nick Flynn. Used by permission of W. W. Norton & Company, Inc.

"The Circle Game" from *The Circle Game* copyright 1966, 1998, 2012 by Margaret Atwood. Reproduced with permission from House of Anansi Press, Toronto. https://houseofanansi.com/.

Karl Meade, from "ana stasis." Used by permission of the author.

Excerpts from *Camber* by Don McKay, copyright 2004 Don McKay. Reprinted by permission of McClelland & Stewart, a division of Penguin Random House Canada Limited. All rights reserved.

Excerpt from *The Folding Cliffs: A Narrative* by W. S. Merwin, copyright 1998 by W. S. Merwin. Used by permission of Alfred A. Knopf, an imprint of the Knopf Doubleday Publishing Group, a division of Penguin Random House LLC. All rights reserved.

"The Night, the Porch," from *Blizzard of One: Poems* by Mark Strand, copyright 1998 by Mark Strand. Used by permission of Alfred A. Knopf, an imprint of the Knopf Doubleday Publishing Group, a division of Penguin Random House LLC. All rights reserved.

For Karl, Georgia, and Stephanie, my whole world.

Thou knowest how poor a trifling thing man is,
And learn'st thus much by our anatomy,
The heart being perished, no part can be free

       —JOHN DONNE
     from "An Anatomy of the World"

Contents

List of Illustrations | xi
Acknowledgements | xiii

1 **Heart** | 1
    Anatomy of the World | 3
    Flood | 6
    My Father Was a Surgeon | 9
    Ice Storm | 11
    The Cupboard | 14
    The Cupboard, Again | 17
    Lost Boy | 19
    Lost Boy, Again | 21

2 **Lungs** | 23
    The Ghost in Me | 25
    The Making of a Poet | 27
    Free | 30
    Falling Down | 33
    Ballad of Lost Causes | 36
    The Present | 38
    Oneiromancy | 41

3 **Liver** | 43
    Hundred-Year-Old House | 45
    Volcano | 48
    Night Ferry | 51
    Tree of Knowledge | 54
    Just Like Your Mother | 57
    By Any Other Name | 60
    It's Not Looking Good | 62
    Straw | 65

4 **Skeleton** | 67
    The Bardo | 69
    Gutter | 72
    Furies | 74
    Ages | 77
    The Ones You Love | 80
    Ventriloquist | 83
    Dear God | 85
    Clam Diggers | 88
    Bright Angel | 91
    Slow Wormes and Glass Lizards | 93

Thank You | 95
Notes | 96

List of Illustrations

Flammarion Wood Engraving, by an unknown artist, published in Camille Flammarion's book of 1888: *L'atmosphere: Meteorologie Populaire*. The engraving itself is probably from the sixteenth century, the time of Donne. The caption in Flammarion's book read: "A traveller puts his head under the edge of the firmament."

China Boat 1998. Oil on board by Celia Meade, collection of The Alberta Foundation for the Arts.

Acknowledgements

THESE POEMS APPEARED, SOME in slightly different form, in the following magazines:

Brushfire, Winter 2020: "Falling Down"

Euphony Journal, February 2020: "Flood"

The Inflectionist Review, May 2021: "The Ghost in Me"

Louisville Review, Spring 2020: "Hundred-Year-Old House"

Opiate, August 2021: "The Ones You Love"

Plainsongs, Winter 2020: "Volcano"

The Rail, February 2022: "Bright Angel" and "The Present"

Whistling Shade, Fall/Winter 2020: "My Father Was a Surgeon"

1
Heart

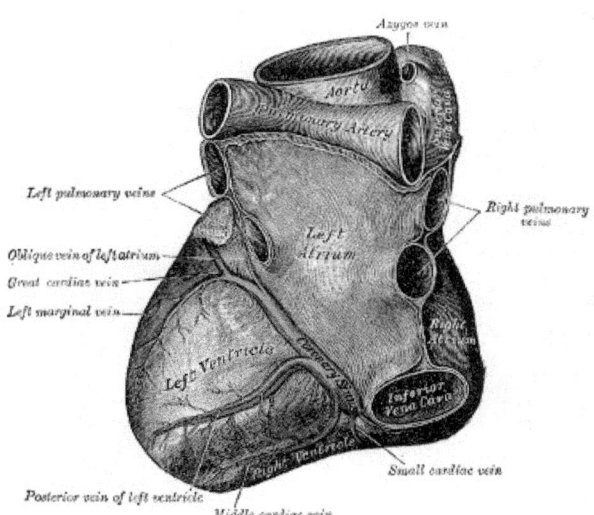

No man is an Island, intire of itselfe; every man is a peece of the Continent, a part of the maine

—JOHN DONNE
from "Devotions upon Emergent Occasions"

Anatomy of the World

How I long to describe the world:
its longitudinal bones, its lava
heart, its forested lungs,
its murk, its swamp liver.

In Revelations
angels herald from
four corners of the earth
but the earth is round.

People walk around this ball
and stick to the underside—
such is the pull
to an unknowable core.

Donne's *Anatomy of the World*
laments a young woman dying
laments the world as a place
that this could happen.

No one hovers above
and you are my angel
on an earth full of
hungry spirits, and ghosts.

The earth whirled.
You felt cornered. I stuck
to you. We meandered down
under; ranged over the continent.

We dwell in our corner,
our island of moss and fog.
Anatomy of the World is
Donne's analysis of the world.

His conclusion: it's all about
love, and dying.
How I love to be with you
long to be, always.

Twice or thrice had I lov'd thee
before I knew thy face or name.[1]
Before you and me, Donne
spoke the landscape of us

how our hearts erupt
and the blood flows
until our day
is done.

---

1. John Donne, "Air and Angels," https://www.poetryfoundation.org/poems/44091/air-and-angels-56d2230aa341c.

Would it have been worth while,
After the sunsets and the dooryards and the sprinkled
        streets,
After the novels, after the teacups, after the skirts that
        trail along the floor—

—T. S. ELIOT
from "The Lovesong of J. Alfred Prufrock"

Flood

Our house sat at the bottom of a hill,
where it all started, where we began,
the ground fertile, but the structure rotten.
It rocked and eventually fell,
the walls crashing outwards towards the neighbors
who luckily had kept their distance.

The hill turned golden in the August sun,
the grass burned dry in the south-facing heat.
Paths crossed its surface like landscape art
worn by dogs and wild hares,
children running between school and home,
and us, as we made our climb.

Fall turned into winter and the snow glare was blinding.
In spring we planted seedlings by a basement window.
They grew giant and heavy with green tomatoes,
protected by a forest of marigolds.
At frost, we tucked them in mudroom drawers.

The tomatoes slowly turned red and edible.
But it wasn't enough.
We longed to be up, on top of the hill,
to look down, as it were,
to own a hallway, an entryway,
not just a mudroom to a vegetable patch.

Wood and nails only last so long.
We were never happier than there, my love,
where hollyhocks grew over our heads
and hid the falling-down fence along the alleyway.
The ground was just too close to the river,
and everything swept away in the flood.

Till a' the seas gang dry, my dear,
And the rocks melt wi' the sun;
I will love thee still, my dear,
While the sands o' life shall run.

—ROBERT BURNS
from "A Red, Red Rose"

My Father Was a Surgeon

Some things have to come out
he'd say, a sack full of stones
or the growth on your forehead
obscuring your sight.

But some things are better left
to carry until you die
—the blood red liver, for instance
overrun with flowering buds.

He kept his
pressed near his heart
a thorny bush
spreading branches inside.

It stayed, *in situ*, with the rest,
his blighted knee, his hands,
his piercing intellect,
his untamable hair.

All of it burned
in the great fire
and then we scattered him
among the roses.

fingered & reaching.
The hands grow in clusters,
one upon the next

> —GENNAROSE NETHERCOTT
> from "The Lumberjack's Dove"

Ice Storm

—after G. Nethercott

I thought my father was a coward
he never said he loved me
but then, in the middle of the night
I realized:
he may not have loved me.

In his dying days
he wrote my mother a letter:
I love you, he said.
So—he knew how, but maybe
he loved only her.

I perceive love
like the weather
friends like mist
children like rain.
My father preferred

clarity: is it broken,
or is it whole? Outside,
heavy rain turns to ice.
The gate latch sits frozen
encapsulated.

On stormy nights like this
my father would pick us up
drive us to his house
and feed me and the girls
then drive us home again.

I decide that is love.
My father
remains mute on the subject.

I walk through the encased garden.
Ice wraps thin branches
like x-rays of fingers
that break and shatter
with their own weight.

Cars drive by, over the crush
and fill the air with pungent pine.

I feel so cold. The ground is slippery
I try to reach out
but can I go on
when my fingers feel
like they've been broken off?

I need to grow new fingers
and again, new fingers
there is no other way
to crack the ice
and unhinge, to open the gate.

I sat like that for about an hour,
trying to think what would come next,
and in my mind, the barefoot doll in her
mother's old yellow nightgown sat and stared
into space as well.

"Why honey, don't you want to get dressed?"

—SYLVIA PLATH
from *The Bell Jar*

The Cupboard

I opened the wooden cupboard
and laid the poems on the bed.
No one sees them as I do,
sees the care,
the hours that I put into them.

I lay myself down on the bed.
I'm OK with it,
it's my best work, but
I'm a housewife
really.

I'm not going to kill myself,
or throw them in the trash,
be so dramatic
but when I die, I can see
that's where they will go.

Like my late father's surgical instruments
that he looked after so carefully.
No one wanted them
and all the bodies that he cut
and stitched
are now dead.

I understand
I am a grown-up
and life is like that.
I wrapped up the papers
and put them back in the cupboard.

But then the cupboard shook
and I had to open it again.

Georgia and Stephanie came home from school
I could hear them laughing and talking
Karl came home from work
important, important work
and they wondered

Where's Mama?
Where is she?
And I was wrapped up
in the cupboard
where they couldn't see me
or hear me at all.

I am inhabited by a cry.
Nightly it flaps out
Looking, with its hooks, for something to love.

—SYLVIA PLATH
from "Elm"

The Cupboard, Again

I opened it in the night.
An oily raven flew in my face,
scratching my chest
and rampaging through the room.

It soiled my clothes, dropping
iridescent feathers:
brilliantine, marvellous
scary as wilderness.

It crashed into the mirror, and then
the windowpane until finally, bleeding,
it smashed through
and away.

Delicately, I lifted the bed covers
so the glass and shit stayed on top
then crept under the weighted blanket
to cover my shivering, naked self.

The cupboard stood open,
ravenous, yawning.
Dark shapes moved
and muttered inside.

I lean to kiss him
He lifts up his face to kiss me—
Why can't I reach him? Why can't he reach me?
In that very touch of the kiss
We vanish from each other—he vanishes
Into the skin of water.

—TED HUGHES
from "Narcissus"

Lost Boy

I took your *Karenina* in the canoe
with my brother, and tipped over
getting out. Your Tolstoy was unreadable,
I was full of remorse.

You travelled to northern Alberta
worked in the Chinchaga Wildland,
and read *Ulysses* by the mirrored water.
The world chose not to reflect you.

The world was opaque, celadon
like the wild Athabasca River.
The meaning is silt
the why is the snowcap.

Our daughters brush their liquid hair and
post on Instagram, for their own reasons.
I studied *The Death of Ivan Ilyich*
you pored over poetry books made delicate

by your affection.
Our son slipped under, we only
glimpsed him: my father's hands,
a flicker of your brother's eyes.

The heart shifts shape of its own accord—
From bird to axe, from pinwheel
to budded branch. It rolls over in the chest,
a brown bear groggy with winter

—DORIANNE LAUX
from "Heart"

Lost Boy, Again

A bird pecks at the window
he wants to snatch
my curly, blonde hair
to line his nest

or maybe he's pissed
I'm sitting so close to his nest
go find some other place to drink coffee
he pecks out in bird code

or he doesn't see through the window at all
and gazes at his own reflection
how lovely, how perfect this strange bird is
and so familiar

or he sees in his reflection
as some aggressive adversary
flying in his territory
audacious, outrageous.

No. It's my dead son
tapping at the window
of his living
breathing mother.

he soars high above
the cacophonous flock
and feasts on arbutus berries
apples, crab apples

left to rot
by me, the neglectful,
sorrowful gardener.

I want him to come back
to regrow in my belly
to be my reflection
with the same blond hair

to relegate him
to life on the ground,
tapping on the computer
in a loop of forgotten passwords.

Why, when he can soar
with his beautiful plumage
free of human
insane pursuits?

Fly hard into that window
see the sky in a pane of glass
burst your berry-sized heart
and die again

come back to me
so I can hold you
so I can hold
your human hand.

2
Lungs

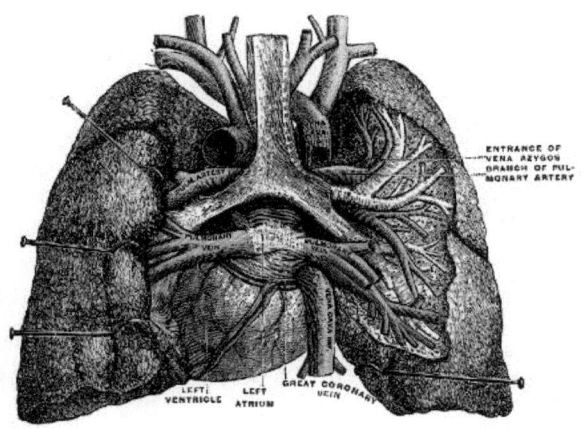

We will be proud of course the air will be
Good for breathing at last

>   —W. S. MERWIN
>   from "When the War Is Over"

The Ghost in Me

```
    Your         hearts         on            branches
       lilac         bob            sinew


scented   candles   stretched   and    dipping into    ruffled
   wicks.     I     carry     the smell    of you    deep    into
                           my    nose,
                          through
                            my
                           wind
                           pipe
                          trunk,
                         through
                         my lung's
                    bronchiole   branches,
                      to their end    in alveoli,
                   empty   flower    buds  of  air.
              I use this ghost       of you to breathe.
              As I need the real you  (my mirror, my true love)
          as your daytime waste, your   oxygen  effuse is my very
life's                                                     breath.
```

I was swinging, out over treetops.
I saw myself never going back, yet
whatever breathed in the mute woods
was not another life.

—JUDITH SLATER
from *Family Vacation*

The Making of a Poet

My mother
loved nothing more than us
growing inside of her
which may explain
the number, the numbers of brothers.

My oldest brother drew maps.
He used screens, he input data
to see the earth in ones and zeros
in geography.

My second brother made rooms
where the walls moved
and his wife ran through the audience
(naked . . . we couldn't listen properly).

He was a set designer
is what I'm trying to tell you
they were theater people
they bore a clown
and a philosopher
—I can't go into that now.

My sister was an intensive care nurse
she specialized in bad veins
they would call for her
from all over the hospital
and my other, little brother
a doctor like my father.

Me, who came before him
I'm random, not sequential
(and actually not that useful)
I started scientific,
slides under a microscope
but I loved to draw

loved lines, the smell of paint
linseed oil and canvas—oh!
I couldn't sleep for the excitement.

Then I got buried in babies and
everyone grew older and
that caused my father to die
and my daughter Georgia to nearly die
and her partner D to drink.

I thought my head would burst
but something else split open
and grew and spread
through my head
down my arm

out the fingers of my left hand
in inky, illegible scrawl
and it was poetry.

Like bodiless water passing in a sigh,
Thro' palsied streets the fatal shadows flow,
And in their sharp disastrous undertow
Suck in the morning sun, and all the sky.

—LOUISE IMOGEN GUINEY
from *Fog*

Free

I dreamed I went travelling,
I carried a heavy suitcase
full of rusted, twisted metal.
"I might need that," D said,

"carry it for me."
I wanted the idea of D,
just not all the rest.
The next night

I sat using a pottery wheel.
A wide shallow bowl emerged,
expansive and smooth.
Then a lump evolved,

and developed into D.
I tried to peel him off with a razor blade,
I had to work fast, before the clay dried.
I worried that the bowl would break,

and a weakness formed, a ripple, a scar.
If only D hadn't formed on my bowl,
I wouldn't have had to do all that cutting.
Freud would have said

that I was female, hollowed out,
and meant to carry others.
But in spite of Freud, in spite of
me and in spite of D,

I want to be free.
I fly through a fog high over the mountains,
below I see glimpses of forest and lake,
if I put anything in my wide smooth bowl,

I want it to be this fog,
to breathe it into my lungs
and leave no trace behind.

Who is the third that walks always beside you?
When I count, there are only you and I together
But when I look ahead up the white road
There is always another one walking beside you

—T. S. ELIOT
from *The Waste Land*

Falling Down

Stephanie can't breathe.
She sits in emerg, with a
man who has a spider in his ear:
trapped, still crawling;

with a carpenter who
sawed off all his fingers;
with a soccer player,
a blood-soaked towel
pressed to her mouth;

with a girl like a porcelain doll
they poke again and again.
It's her mother's face
that makes me cry.

My daughter dons a mask.
Steam pours in her mouth
to coax open
her bloody-minded lungs.

An old woman lies on a gurney:
All I did was fall down.

A wife says good-bye to her husband
as he wheels into the O.R.
they sob and clutch each other
then she walks out alone.

We walk out together
into the night
while a figure stares at us
from the forest edge.

Oh dream, why do you do me this way?
Again, with the digging, again with the digging up.
Once more with the shovels.
Once more, the shovels full of dirt.

—DIANE SUESS
from "Ballad"

Ballad of Lost Causes

So Georgia gets expelled
so she never finished high school
so her man (a hella drinker)
gets charged with punching out a cop

and then Stephanie's suspended
and she sits at home to study
and friends come around to visit
and the dog jumps on the sofa

and their kid is in med school
or ensconced in some castle
and yes, I have an awesome husband
and some hella awesome wheels

but the door is frozen shut
and the car needs towing to Vancouver
and the Starbucks at the airport
seems to have closed, for good

I went to the wrong taxi stand
not international departures
and the float plane limped low
over Active Pass

just under the pressing fog.

what is left is a beak,
a wing,
a sense of feathers,

—LINDA PASTAN
from "Memory of a Bird"

The Present

You gave me
an egg holder:
antique, made of wood
made of holes

each one awaiting
an egg. Not
practical, now, to keep
eggs on the counter

but that was then: and like our words
it was prone to splinter
spiked with nails, seeping
angry metal stains

now a useless
unwanted thing.
There are no chickens here
and you didn't last either.

You chose the air
where the egg was to sit.
I burnt the gift in the hearth.
At present it holds nothing.

But I remember—do you—
when we thought the present held us
each in our brittle, fragile shells—
before the stray downy feather,
before the dark drop of blood.

I cannot remember when it began. The lights were low. We were walking across the floor, over polished wood and inlaid marble, through shallow water, through dustings of snow, through cloudy figures of fallen light. I cannot remember, but I think you were there, whoever you were.

—MARK STRAND
in The Delirium Waltz.

Oneiromancy

Here is the dream:

my parents urged me
to have a party
then they went upstairs
and the yelling began

my gay best friend
sat flounced in pink
You can't be my friend, he shouted,
while you're still friends with her!

I wanted him gone
my parents would wake
(although my mother is stone deaf
and my father is long dead).

In steamy August
the fan swooped
a lopsided swish
and dawn pierced the blinds

distant murmurs
droned from my daughter's room
until my husband yelled
go to sleep!

Who was the gay best friend?
Was it the bird at dawn
or the menacing wind
that blew up after midnight?

Oneiromancy
the divination of dreams
my word of the day
from Merriam Webster

You'll never use that word,
Stephanie muttered.
So wrong, I thought,
so, so wrong.

3
Liver

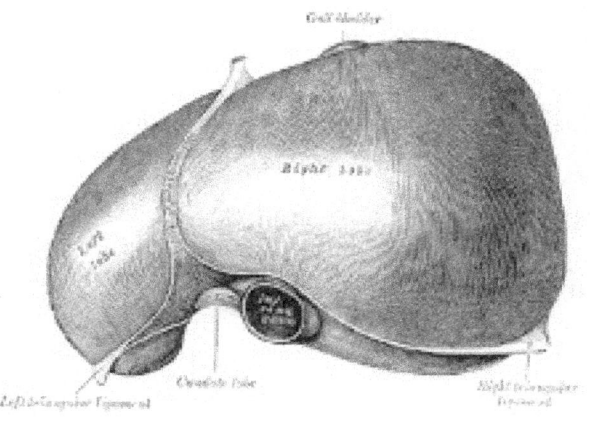

a mirrored flickering across the cold waters.
We allow ourselves the crest that breaks
above the surface then re-forms.

We make it human and we call it love.
This wintering is my own and not the world's,
although the world is wintering.

—PETER SACKS
from "Night Ferry"

Hundred-Year-Old House

At dawn, Georgia called.
D had been up all night drinking,
her friend cowered under the kitchen table,
her new friend Marguerite,
who had nowhere else to go.

He pushed her, he slapped her hand.
Drive away, I said,
go to your grandmother's.
But she's afraid D might do something,
she's afraid he'll go to work.

He's outside naked
wandering up the road.
Now he's coiling the hose around his neck.
We sit on another island,
our stomachs turn to stone.

Our house is one hundred years old.
A Garry oak tree out back
fans out over the morning light
in a halo of pink and orange.
Evergreens shelter us from the north wind.

I brush back the yellow silk curtain,
where the dog chewed the bottom corner,
the dog, so beautiful, but not above eating drywall.
Not above leaping to the counter
and snatching the packet of salmon.

These troubles occupied my mind
before she called and reminded me
that I didn't have problems,
only a silky dog, yellow curtains
and a lack of dinner plans.

We get on the ferry and drive,
look out for her, for signs,
but she has left,
driving him home,
driving Marguerite to the bus stop.

She comes back. Hours pass.
She wants to see him, but we won't give her the keys.
I have to see him, she said, as the cab drove away.
This is about love, she said.
You don't understand.

nothing cures. An immense slackening ache, as when,
thawing, the rigid landscape weeps

—PHILIP LARKIN
from *Faith Healing*

Volcano

I remember when you lived with us,
your easy smile, the missing teeth concealed,
your blond hair and giant, gentle hands.
You spread out from a chair as if still growing
even though you were thirty
and all your growing was done.

You'd come home laughing
I was only a little bit bad, you said.
Held up by the wall
until you slid down to the floor in the laundry room.
I tried to kick you out
but you gave me a roll of hot, sweaty bills, and that was that.

We lived that way for some time,
mashed potatoes and ground beef,
curry made you sick, the smell of it.
You'd come home laughing,
but then you'd come home shaking
and need gas money so you could go to work.

Our pretty balcony
in the sunshine, the view
gradually obscured by beer cans, the drain clogged by butts
until it became a puddle of misery on the second floor.
You had to go, but you had no place to go.
We stood for a while, unmoving.

I remember when you lived with us,
your wide mouth, your soft hair and strong body,
you poured out on the chair like molten lava,
a smoking, drinking volcano,
but you melted, eroded,
and finally washed away.

Its clean air winnowed by angels ; she has come
Back to her early sea-town home
Scathed, stained after tedious pilgrimages.
Barefoot, she stood, in shock of that returning

—SYLVIA PLATH
from "Dream with Clam-Diggers"

Night Ferry

I woke up and shuffled to unload the dishes,
but in their place was a rack of hardcover books.
They had been washed and dried,
bleached clean and warm.

I tried to write about truth
but it became filled with D's bottles
and other failings and irritations,
the smallish parameters of my heart.

I yearned to clean it all up
in a special censorious machine.
No damage to poetry, no hurt feelings,
just us, sanitized into a warm, perfect creation.

Outside in the blue, swirling snow
Georgia dreamed she was high up in the mountains
but she had a morning shift, she couldn't be late again,
so she drove all night over the pass.

She headed down into the valley, towards the sea.
Boarding the ferry, she walked the outer decks, the various lounges.
When, when will this ferry arrive? Seven o'clock, someone finally told her.
She woke with a start, and it was seven o'clock.

That night, you dreamed too of the mountains.
You were at obedience class,
high up in a stone castle, awaiting the instructor.
You gradually became aware that there weren't any dogs.

Obedience is not a strong family trait,
we crush to get through the door all at once.
Wait your turn, but it's my turn now,
now, *now*

You wanted to be born; I let you be born.
When has my grief ever gotten
In the way of your pleasure?
Plunging ahead
into the dark and light at the same time
Eager for sensation
As though you were some new thing, wanting

—LOUISE GLUCK
from *End of Winter*

Tree of Knowledge

Just after spring equinox, we walk down to the main road at dusk.
Clouds scud past the mountain as you slip and fall.

I watch, unable to help you. The moon hangs a curved dagger
as I walk home alone, where white flowers appear, shimmering

in bloom before their leaves unfurl. Magnolia: here before bees,
their petals tough enough to withstand pollinating beetles.

When we first came, I was captivated by the magnolia in the garden
arching its petals over the weathered grey house.

A woman died in her sleep here, before her children were grown—
the stage already set for tragedy. The year we took possession

I raked uncured manure, steaming, over the soil. Such was
my ambition, to create something better.

The magnolia tree was burned. It had survived ice ages,
mountain-building, continental drift: 95 million years

to meet its end under my care. I planted again and watered
the flowering bushes that now crowd our front step.

Trumpets of magnolia, the first flowers:
to evolve in our world, the first to bloom in spring.

The old house leaks into various buckets
impressed that it has survived a century

but like so many things humans built and invented
we interfered with something we didn't understand.

You sleep in late after skidding home.
I walk into town, feeling helpless.

I find market strawberries, the first, soft fruit of summer
and eucalyptus fronds with their pungent, healing scent.

It's going to be okay. Will everything be okay?
I cut back branches so we can get to the door.

We'll live this way for a few years longer.

We think that the point is to pass the test or to overcome the problem, but the truth is that things don't really get solved. They come together and they fall apart. Then they come together again and fall apart again. It's just like that.

—PEMA CHODRON
from *The Pocket Pema Chodron*

Just Like Your Mother

A couple sat behind me on the plane
with a diaper bag and a boy.
He kicked the seat
as soon as they sat down.

"Control your child," I said.
I never could control
what came out of my mouth.
When Georgia was six

she put on three layers of clothes
and walked away.
A cop said: *What will you do
when she's sixteen?*

On her sixteenth birthday
she spent the night
with a couple—teenage runaways
on someone else's boat.

The boy tried to kiss her
then the girl
punched my child in the nose
and stole her clothes.

I found her
holding herself, dirty
lined up for the restroom
in Centennial Park.

I drove her to school
to sit her final exam.
She walked in the front door
and out the back.

In a house where the floor
was covered in human hair
she asked a woman, too drunk
to get up from her chair

Will you be my mother?
My child told me that.
She never could control
what came out of her mouth.

O, train me not, sweet mermaid, with thy note,
To drown me in thy sister's flood of tears:
Sing, siren, for thyself, and I will dote:
spread o'er the silver waves thy golden hairs,
and as a bed I'll take them, and there lie;
And in that glorious supposition, think
He gains by death that has such means to die

       —SHAKESPEARE
      from *The Comedy of Errors*

By Any Other Name

Your birth mother named you
Rhiannon, queen of hell
but we named you again
Georgia, lover of earth
I, whose name means blindness

thought we could rewrite this story
with lines cobbled together.
Hell on earth, queen of lovers,
I stumble to lead you through the dark.

I want to cast down
those who would hurt you
build a force field around you
but you already feel too alone.

You wish to be pierced
by all comers,
to experience every cut,
every goddamned thing.

This is your desire:
to mix your blood
become joined to it again,
married to the Earth, as one.

The night he showed us his photo album, after the house went quiet, I crept into the kitchen for a glass of water, the sink still full of sea clams, forgotten under the fluorescent hum. They'd opened their shells and were waving their feet, each as thick and long as my forearm. A box of snakes, some draped on to the countertop, some trying to pull themselves out.

—NICK FLYNN
from *Another Bullshit Night in Suck City*

It's Not Looking Good

Kicked out of beauty school
Georgia smokes in bed.
Everyone is dressed for Easter
in pretty pastel clothes.

Not everyone. Georgia's in
her robe and nightie
in twisted sheets and
heavy blankets.

Meanwhile, I can't get
this sweater off
it's too small
and too tight.

When Georgia was small,
she was exquisite
and I dressed her
in beautiful clothes.

She gets out of bed
only to lock her keys in the car.
I've combed my hair
to go to the damn party.

It's fine, she said later, over the phone.
She lives at the end of a dead-end street.
She broke the smallest car window
and taped it shut with cardboard.

Now that I've put on this sweater
I have to figure my own way out.

Yet he despises them: they are so
Victorian Christmas-card:
the cheap paper shows
under the pigments of
their cheerful fire-
places and satin
ribboned suburban laughter
and they have their own forms
of parlour
games: father and mother
playing father and mother

He's glad
to be left
out by himself
in the cold

—MARGARET ATWOOD
from "The Circle Game"

Straw

They're lucky, you said, as they fell,
the drunken skiers, slipping on their
ski boot feet. We sat in candlelight
with a fondue warmed between us

and I saw we were
a house of straw.
I wanted to believe
that straw could turn to gold.

I wanted that kind of power,
to make you sober
and make you want
to be sober. You wanted

enchantment, to light matches
and drop them while I slept
the deep sleep of fables. We were
not in the same story.

I thought we were the lucky ones.
You danced around
the firemen in your stockinged feet
Hope less you sang out

just before you vanished.
Why can't I write my own
happy ending? I was not aware
this story was a tragedy.

You remain with the bottle
your one true love
and I keep Georgia,
the firstborn child

—perhaps that is the happy ending.

4
Skeleton

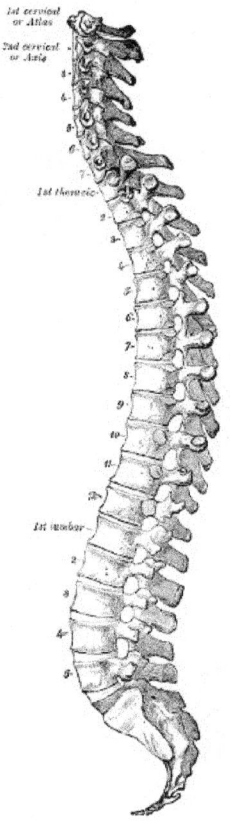

Extinguish my eyes, I can still see you,
Close my ears, I can hear your footsteps fall

> —RAINER MARIA RILKE
> from *The Book of Pilgrimage*
> trans. by Jessie Lamont.

The Bardo

The boat was small.
My father
on the rocky shore,
anxious but silent.
A dog swam alongside me
as we moved
across a cold, windy harbor.

The boat was small,
but I sat erect
felt sure it would carry me across.
My spine bowed, however,
as the shore receded.
The dog sank under choppy waters.

The shore was desolate,
empty, gravelly.
My skin prickled as my father
stood and wrung his hands.
The drowning dog
made me understand.
This journey in the sturdy boat
was the same one as the dog, as all dogs.

The wind blew,
the water icy
and the shore approached.
The boat
no comfort.
Eventually
I would arrive.

she and i
one stroke after another
crawl cross the water
he and she through

—KARL MEADE
from *ana stasis*

Gutter

I was scooping out the gutters,
as the rain pissed down,
water launched off the roof
like a goddamn feature fountain

Somehow I
extracted out whatever
nasty thing was stuck there
(dead rat, a dead squirrel)

as I chatted on the telephone
(miraculous, impossible)
to my father.
Dad, is that you?
he only grunted

because you know,
I stuttered, blushing
you are dead
The phone clicked silent
and I clung to the rungs

of the vertiginous ladder
tall and slick enough
to reach the waterfall.

The breath whose might I have invoked in song
Descends on me; my spirit's bark is driven,
Far from the shore, far from the trembling throng
Whose sails were never to the tempest given;
The massy earth and sphered skies are riven!
I am borne darkly, fearfully, afar

—PERCY BYSSHE SHELLEY
from *Adonais*

Furies

—after Marie Howe

I put too much chili in the chili
put a plastic bowl in the oven
I harangued the Home Depot clerk
and stuck my arm through the subway door.

I cried when the train conductor
had me put the dog on the floor.
I yelled at the twelve-year-old
who had yelled at my ten-year-old.

I pushed the wrong button
and the elevator door closed.
My daughter skipped school
so I conducted her
from classroom to classroom.

Then the feckless boy
abandoned our canoe
and I heard a roaring
a rushing in my ear
a fury

I stepped alone, into the red canoe
without a life jacket, in high winds,
and wheeled around and around
like a red second hand
on a giant clock
spinning out to sea.

To die with style:
As the tree retreats inside itself,
shutting off the valves at its
extremities
                to starve in technicolor, then
Having served two hours in a children's leaf pile, slowly
stir its vitamins into the earth.

                            —DON MCKAY
                from "Some Functions of a Leaf"

Ages

Feet grow too far
away for socks, hands:
balloon animals.

I walk in the rain
by a hawk in the ditch
where a dead rabbit lay.

At home, I hear you talk
through a wall, but you stand
right in front of me.

Night static hisses and
I read to stop my mind racing
but my eyes are dry.

Your father looks at me in anger
or shame—I guess
because he can't talk

or use the toilet
or walk. I'm coming
to meet you, father-in-law

the earth calls us all down
to disintegrate, to dissolve
into the rainy ditch

where the hawk will find us
if we're not burnt to ash first
lovingly annihilated
and scattered in the sea.

They sat with him until morning
and then they took him up to a small cave hidden
in a buttress at the base of the cliff and they dug
a grave for him inside it and lined it with ferns

       —W. S. MERWIN
      from "The Folding Cliffs"

The Ones You Love

—after Aaron Caycedo-Kimura

What if you promised
you would kill me
the night before I was taken
to the care home, or to the hospice?

What if I asked you to
grind a pill into my evening
glass of milk—
is that love?

He spoke of the mother
who asked her son
to carry her to the mountain
and leave her in an earthen hollow.

His own parents did not want
any notice given
upon their death
just as my parents wanted.

Is this humility
or is it the mother
calling them back?
Back to the great glowing

of those who were separate
but exist now—
together
in their far-off mountain womb.

"Poor Pinocchio! I really pity you!"
"Why do you pity me?"
"Because you are a puppet and, what is worse, because you have a wooden head."

—CARLO COLLIDI
from *Pinocchio*

Ventriloquist

I am the dummy
and my body is a puppet
I need your hand to fill me
and to sit me on your lap.

My voice is yours
you speak through me
my jaw goes up and down as if
I have something to say

as if you would mock me, Master,
although you gave me life and breath
as if you yearn for audience
to laugh at my expense.

Give me something
important to say
the show is almost over:
give me something,

give me anything

I'm dying here

Much Gesture, from the Pulpit—
Strong Hallelujahs roll—
Narcotics cannot still the Tooth
That nibbles at the soul—

—EMILY DICKENSON
from "This World Is Not Conclusion"

Dear God

You, who inhabit all of Creation
but use the Western Wall
as Your personal mailbox,
I deliver this letter to You.
I would like to call attention
to my particular burdens:

my dog is so wired
she jumps up on everyone
and my husband and mother
are going deaf, so require
me to repeat myself
to always repeat myself.

As You well know
I recently fell and smacked my face
(tripped over a tree root)
on the pavement.
My tooth rolled out:
an expensive gold crown

I said Your name
in vain several times,
several times.

So much blood and humiliation
only steps away from Your house!
Where I had attended
a bell-ringing concert
that left me touched
by Your Presence:

What's the message?
Write me, if You could
and explain, please explain.
Sincerely, Yours

To stare at nothing is to learn by heart
What all of us will be swept into, and baring oneself
To the wind is feeling the ungraspable somewhere close by.

—MARK STRAND
from *The Night, the Porch*

Clam Diggers

Happisburgh, on the foreshore
by a changing Norfolk coastline,
a family of footprints appeared
800,000 years old.
Footprints in sand, wet by the ocean

outlast by millennia the feet
that made them, revealed to future
strangers, shod in Nikes and tube socks.

They were probably clamming
like my father loved to,
tipping back one clam after another,
squelching in the wet boundary
between ocean and land.

To see those footprints
was to press your own toes
in the sand. I felt crabs escape
beneath my bare feet.

Fans poured plaster casts and
photographed trace fossils of
their ancient fathers, ancient
mothers.

The monkey in Perth Zoo,
pressed her hand against Stephanie's
across the gulf of species
to show that in essence
our experience is the same.

At the earth's imagin'd corners, blow
Your trumpets, Angels, and arise, arise

—JOHN DONNE
from "Holy Sonnets"

Bright Angel

Bright Angel Park, deep in the rainforest
where the Cowichan River cuts musical curves
where a bridge hangs to dance across
and a rope swing swings

over deep river grooves
in the pine-scented shadows.
I took my girls there
to be cool in hot weather.

I see Georgia swaying, standing in water
and the wet ripples emanate away, away
like a record, a 45 that plays out her life
while Stephanie hangs in the air

between rope and river
like a treble note trilling away, away . . .
Oh, that beautiful time in the heat of the summer
when the children were shining, shining with light.

The heart closes its doors, becomes smoke,
a wispy lie, curls like a worm and forgets
its life, burrows into the fleshy dirt.

—DORIANNE LAUX
from *Heart*

Slow Wormes and Glass Lizards

—*after* Steven Buczacki's *Fauna Britannica*

Glimmer of light in the shade of the garden,
a being of many names: glass lizard
death-adder, slow worme.
No arms or legs

it's a snake with eyelids
a snake that blinks
and eats slugs for supper
oh horror, the horror, and yet

it lives for decades
in the garden,
where it witnesses birds
braiding the air with song

where the moon is its timepiece
with its numberless white face
(like the slow worme, without hands)
reflecting light from the sun.

Our brilliant sun cannot
be looked at, or approached
without death
yet—is the mother of us all.

I slow down to lay in the grass,
slow enough to hear my heart
now, now, now
and I think yes, this is living

I think of my arms and legs,

how I hold on too tight at times,
and other times run away.
The slow worme will part
with its tail if it must

I envy its ability to let go.
And why can't I braid us:
slow worme, the moon, and me
into a higher self?

A silver being who can hold on gently,
braid fingers, and feel a soaring
love: blinding, shimmering,
fragile, but not breaking.

Thank You

I AM GRATEFUL TO Sarah Lawrence College and their Masters in Creative Writing, for which I prepared this manuscript as thesis for Professor Dennis Nurkse. Thank you, Dennis, for guiding me in large ways and small, by suggesting books to study for their format, and line editing each poem in three subsequent drafts. You gave me solid constructive criticism and encouragement both.

I applied to Sarah Lawrence to study under Marie Howe after reading "What the Living Do." I thank her for her guidance and for all of her beautiful and moving books. Thank you, Afaa Micheal Weaver, teacher, author of "The Government of Nature," for your generous reading of a chapbook version preceding this manuscript.

Thank you to my writing group: Barbara Lock, Janet Pfeffer, Tessa Rossi, Jeanne Marie Fleming, and Erin Swanson, SLC MFA grads and wonderful Editors and teachers all, who helped me shape many of these poems.

Thank you to Sharon Olds for her masterpiece *Stag's Leap*, and Nick Flynn for his memoir *Another Bullshit Night in Suck City* and his many lovely books of poetry. I bow down to you both.

Thank you to my amazing mother Beryl Scott and my brilliant father Gerald Scott. I miss and love him so much.

Thank you to my partner Karl, who made notes on this manuscript and on every poem as I wrote it. First reader, fellow adventurer in the world of poetry, I love and honor you.

Thank you to my beautiful daughters Georgia and Stephanie, whom along with their father are my whole world, whom I love so much and who allowed their real names to be used in this book.

Notes

THIS BOOK IS A collection of confessional poems about my world, told through the anatomy of family life. It takes its name from Donne's poem, written in 1611, entitled "An Anatomy of the World," which was commissioned upon the death of a fourteen-year-old girl, "wherein . . . the frailty and decay of this whole world is represented."[1] Quotes from Donne and others are interspersed throughout, creating a dialogue.

My girls read this book and gave it a pass to publish, so long as I don't get famous.

JUST LIKE YOUR MOTHER

Georgia quibbled with the facts in this poem. She was punched in the nose at a party in the hills and not on a boat on her birthday. When I picked her up at the boat and drove her to her final exam, she went in and wrote the exam and got 67 percent, in spite of not attending class or handing in assignments. I said she walked out the other door in the poem as a shorthand way of saying she dropped out of high school.

HUNDRED-YEAR-OLD HOUSE
This is Georgia's favorite poem.

---

1. John Donne, *Anatomy of the World: Wherein by Occasion of the Untimely Death of Mistris Eliz. Drury the Frailty and Decay of This Whole World Is Represented* (London: Macham, 1612).

BY ANY OTHER NAME
Georgia did not want me to use pseudonyms in the book because we would have had to remove this poem. It uses the meaning of our actual names:
Georgia: earth-lover
Rhiannon: queen of Hell
Celia: blindness

FREE
This poem is from the imagined viewpoint of Georgia.

SLOW WORMES AND GLASS LIZARDS
When in elementary school, Georgia borrowed *Fauna Britannica* from our neighbor Jack Albhouse. She promptly ripped the cover, so I replaced his copy and kept the book. Once again, I have Georgia to thank for poetic inspiration, in the form of this lovely encyclopedia.

www.ingramcontent.com/pod-product-compliance
Lightning Source LLC
Chambersburg PA
CBHW071717040426
42446CB00011B/2109